RELAXING LANDSCAPES

REVERSE COLORING BOOK

Enjoying this book?

Please leave a review because we would love to know your thoughts, feedback, and opinions to create better paper products for you!

Thank you so much for your support.

Made in United States
Orlando, FL
09 December 2024

55238406R00057